Experimenting with Everything

Gabrielle Hunter

Experimenting with Everything © 2023
Gabrielle Hunter

All rights reserved.

Presentation by *BookLeaf Publishing*

Web: www.bookleafpub.com

E-mail: info@bookleafpub.com

ISBN: 9789357440561

First edition 2023

*Dedicated to my dad because I've always
wanted to be a writer like he was (even if it was
just the highschool newspaper)*

ACKNOWLEDGEMENT

To my close friends and family

PREFACE

I've always joked about publishing poetry and am just so thankful to actually be able to do this. My life truly is a dream.

I am a poet

i am a poet
but so is everyone
because poetry is nothing
but the organization of words
and it can be abstract
so the concept
of art is really
the conceptualization
of the beautification
and the romantisizing
of nothing

what is life?

what is life
scientifically it is when something is living
but what is the point
if the goods are outnumbered
by the miseries
why do we want to stay alive

why do we choose life
when we could easily take our own
through hard times we hope it gets better
but what if it never does?
what if there is no more happiness
just misery
why should i choose to live
my life isnt crucial to yours
my life is nothing
it could be taken from me at any moment
and i wouldnt be sad
i wouldnt feel anything
i would be dead

no more misery
no more happiness
just dead
maybe death is the right choice

but we dont know it yet
you only get one shot at life
but then you get to choose when you die

but if you die
you cant come back
there isnt anything else
no happiness
no misery
no life
nothing

so although
being dead
doesnt seem too bad
its giving up
what you could have had
what you could have made
what you could have become

i saw some frogs today
four to be exact
they werent alive
but they were still frogs
they were still frogs
but i couldnt keep them as a pet
i couldnt admire them hopping
i couldnt listen to their croak

they were dead
in the street
flat, smushed, dead
so life is a thing that can be taken
at any point of time
someone could put a gun to my head
and then i would, too be dead
it wouldnt be my choice
i would choose to live
but what do i care
im dead

if i were a fly

if i were a fly
then id fly way up high
to feel like im my-
self i lie down in the grass and think
what if this is it

the wind the water the trees
none of them matter to me
but they are all important
without them, i wouldnt be

so i fly and i fly
until i get too high
and i feel so small
and i want to cry
but my eyes run dry
and my stomach is tied

and i fall

The World is so Small

i took two steps around it and was back where i
began
i wish that were reality but there's so much going
on
i feel like i can never grasp what's happening all
at once
maybe it's because i'm not attentive and just
need to sit and watch
or maybe cause there really is just too much
going on
too much happening, the birds, the trees, the
falls
that's enough in itself, this round earth
and us people we came and just expanded that
"when something is not broken, you shouldn't
try to fix it"
so why did we change so much to attend to our
preferences
when we already change to fit it perfectly
the gears in our bodies tuning in to the curves of
this planet
we adapt, sure it takes time but it's alright by me
im enjoying my life, trying to enjoy me

dreaming in my room

My belongings lay in a cluttered pile
in the center of my floor.
My bedside table is just books
stacked more and more.
And here I sit, all the while,
staring at the wall -
it's deep blue color, like the ocean,
and I start to fall.
To fall asleep: asleep to fall
It's all so nice to me.
My dreams are my presents
underneath my evergreen tree.
And then I think "Well, what are dreams?
Are they just gifts to me?"
My life's a dream, so I guess
My life's a mystery.

I Can Breathe the Water

I'm looking out the window, at one big tree
I'm trying to live- to live a life on land
When I can breathe the water.
No one else can.
I don't think they've even tried.
I don't want to be different,
I don't want to try
I don't want to smuggle the seas under the table
But I do.
I pour water on my bed, on the floor in my room
to make it more comfortable.
The sun dries the drops of the morning dew
I never wear a raincoat and I shower twice a day
My water is my sanctuary and my glass is my
place.

Lunar eclipse in May

it's so beautifully still and silent
the absence of voices fill my soul as soon as i
shut my front door
i feel so alone but in the best way
like i am free of everyone else in the world
and though the occasional car drives by
it's not enough to interfere
with the insanity and moonlight that i bask in

I want to be the moon

i think that i want to be the moon
the way that she seems so sad when i cry
they way she floats so beautifully along the river
the way i am not nearly as elegant
but the way that i want to be

the way that i would dance
and spin around everyone else
and they would all go out at night
and glance up to see me
and sit down to watch and adore
as i shine through their thin blue curtains
because the moon is so beautiful
she's who i want to be

Meaning

that grass is green
but what does that mean
why do words mean certain things
why do countries have a queen and king
why do i sit here and write this thing?

why do i think?
why do i talk?
why do i like things?
why do i not?

what is the cause for everything happening
is it really that important
for me to do these things
i just want to exist
but instead i sit and ween
about what words mean

I am a listener

i love to listen
i listen to stories
i listen to rants
i listen to things people say
and i think in my head
what my response would be (bay)
but i don't say it out loud
because i just like to listen
i sit and intake
all this information
all about the people around me
and their opinions and preferences
and i nod my little head
whether i agree or not
it doesn't really matter because
i am a listener

open a window

they say the grass is greener on the other side
but have they ever been?
ive heard stories
telling me to wait
that it gets better than from after eight
but what do they know
they dont live my life
i know ill never be
something great

but just close the curtains
and take the windows off
go where you cant be seen
and take a night
where you dont have to be clean
nobody will know
they cant peer into your life
through the windows or the door
you can be safe here with your
self

I am bread

i feel like a loaf of bread
and there is a single slice taken out of me
and that slice is going to be toasted
and covered with strawberry jam

i feel like an egg that's been
cracked open
and cooked
and served on the side of my toast

i feel like the china
the fancy glass plate
gotten down from the cabinet
for this special day

i feel like myself
my hunger is true
but i will be fulfilled
and i will feel new

Pomegranates

i eat the seeds
small, red, and beady.
they're bursting gemstones
that taste like summer and fall
and winter and spring all
at once.
their deep color
and flavor in a bite.
i feel so rich
with them filling me.
a magenta globe:
the world in my hands.
i crack it open
and i eat the seeds.

Mixing Day and Night in Me

everyone is like the daytime sun
or like the moon at night
but what about me?
i'm the dusk and dawn
when the moon and sun can talk
and they share a space.
they paint the sky rainbow
and they give me all their colors.
their oranges and pinks
and blues and blacks.
i'm the light of day and beauty of night.
i've been gifted all these things
but still don't fit right.

population at eight billion

the population hit eight billion
just ten days after my birthday
it took a bat and swung
and when the ball came, it struck.
struck like lightning
in an empty field.
what was the effect?
i don't know.
but i'm sure it left a mark,
or at least caused a shock

Birds

Up in the sky
and tucked in the trees
I listen to them chirp
and embrace the cool autumn breeze

I walk and I talk
to myself in my head.
Only the birds can hear,
but I hear them instead

My unspoken friends,
though they are not silent
I tell them my problems
until the day ends

Then I walk back home,
silently, and alone
though they still surround me,
it feels they are gone.

If I were a Book

I'm like a book
full of stories- fact and fiction
but you can't learn anything without opening it-
me
I remain guarded by the hardback covers
that I call my thoughts
not locked away,
just closed to the casual passer-by.
only opened by the occasional interest sparked.
And then closed again.
Destined to wait for the next

I'd answer any question
that I knew the answer to
All I need is someone to ask it.
I don't mind really
it's comfortable on the shelf
gives me time to think-
but now my book is full
and nobody is reading it.

Perspective

I look around and try to romantisize
something. Anything.
The music, the color, the routine,
the dark black coffee sitting by my feet.
but it's all dull.
it makes it easier.
"What is romance without heartache?"
I ask the world as if it cares.
That doesn't matter and neither do I
or maybe I do.
That's the lure, the enticement,
The force thay compells me to go on.
If you knew the ending to a story,
would you still read it?
I ask a new: "Do I have a happy ending?"
But the truth is I don't
I don't. have an ending.
To stop would be to decide.
What a dull, short life.
So I trudge through the flowers
Only seeing storms,
because
"the grass is greener on the other side"
but the petals look much more vibrant
with rain.